FLAGS
STICKER BOOK

Lisa Miles

Edited by Sarah Khan
Designed by Candice Whatmore

Flag images by World Flag Pictures, Chester (UK)
Map illustrations by Craig Asquith/European Map Graphics Ltd

Consultant: Jos Poels
With thanks to William Crampton

How to use this book

There are two hundred different flags in this book. Using the pale flag guides, find the right sticker to go with each flag and then find its country on the map. You will see a date below each national flag. This is the date when the current flag was adopted. You can also use this book as a spotter's handbook to make a note of the flags you have seen.

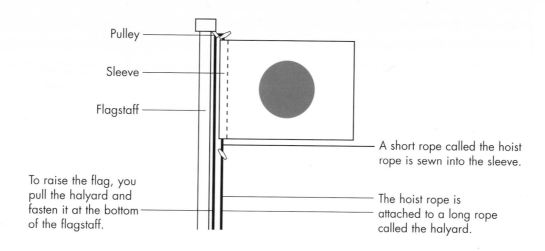

Pulley

Sleeve

Flagstaff

A short rope called the hoist rope is sewn into the sleeve.

To raise the flag, you pull the halyard and fasten it at the bottom of the flagstaff.

The hoist rope is attached to a long rope called the halyard.

This diagram shows how a flag is attached to a pole, or flagstaff.

FLAGS OF THE WORLD

Most of the flags in this book are national flags – they represent one of the world's countries. Some flags, such as those on this page, represent other things. The European flag represents a continent, the Hong Kong flag represents a region in China. The flags of the United Nations, the Red Cross, the Red Crescent and NATO* all represent international organizations.

Front and back

Flags have a front, called the obverse, and a back, called the reverse. The obverse is the side you see when the pole, or flagstaff, is on the left. All the flags in this book show the obverse. The reverse side of a flag is usually a mirror image of the obverse.

The obverse side of the flag of Berlin, Germany's capital. The bear is facing to the left.

The reverse side of the same flag. The bear is facing to the right.

United Nations

DATE	07/08/14
PLACE	New York

Hong Kong

DATE	
PLACE	

Europe

DATE	
PLACE	

NATO*

DATE	
PLACE	

Red Cross

DATE	
PLACE	

Red Crescent

DATE	
PLACE	

*North Atlantic Treaty Organization

AFRICA

Facts and figures

Area:
30.3 million square km
(11.7 million square miles)

Total population:
1 billion*

Largest country: Algeria
381.7 square km
(919.5 sq miles)

Smallest country: Seychelles
445 square km
(176 square miles)

Highest peak: Mount
Kilimanjaro, Tanzania
5,895m (19,241ft)

Longest river:
Nile, Egypt/Sudan
6,671km (4,145 miles)

Biggest city: Cairo, Egypt
Population 15.4 million †

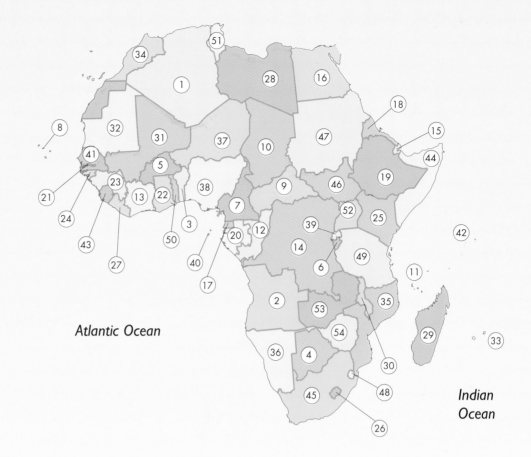

Atlantic Ocean

Indian Ocean

Algeria

① July 3, 1962

DATE	
PLACE	

Angola

② November 11, 1975

DATE	
PLACE	

Benin

③ August 1, 1990

DATE	
PLACE	

Botswana

④ September 30, 1966

DATE	
PLACE	

Burkina Faso

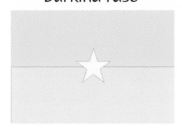

⑤ August 4, 1984

DATE	
PLACE	

Burundi

⑥ June 28, 1967

DATE	
PLACE	

*Source: Population Reference Bureau, www.prb.org
†Source: www.citypopulation.de

AFRICA

Cameroon

⑦ May 20, 1975

DATE	
PLACE	

Cape Verde

⑧ September 25, 1992

DATE	
PLACE	

Central African Rep.*

⑨ December 1, 1958

DATE	
PLACE	

Chad

⑩ November 6, 1959

DATE	
PLACE	

Comoros

⑪ December 23, 2001

DATE	
PLACE	

Congo

⑫ June 10, 1991

DATE	
PLACE	

Côte d'Ivoire

⑬ December 3, 1959

DATE	
PLACE	

Dem. Rep. of Congo†

⑭ February 20, 2006

DATE	
PLACE	

Djibouti

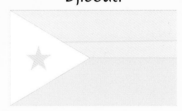

⑮ June 27, 1977

DATE	
PLACE	

Egypt

⑯ October 4, 1984

DATE	
PLACE	

Equatorial Guinea

⑰ October 12, 1968

DATE	
PLACE	

Eritrea

⑱ May 24, 1993

DATE	
PLACE	

*Central African Republic
†Democratic Republic of Congo (formerly Zaire)

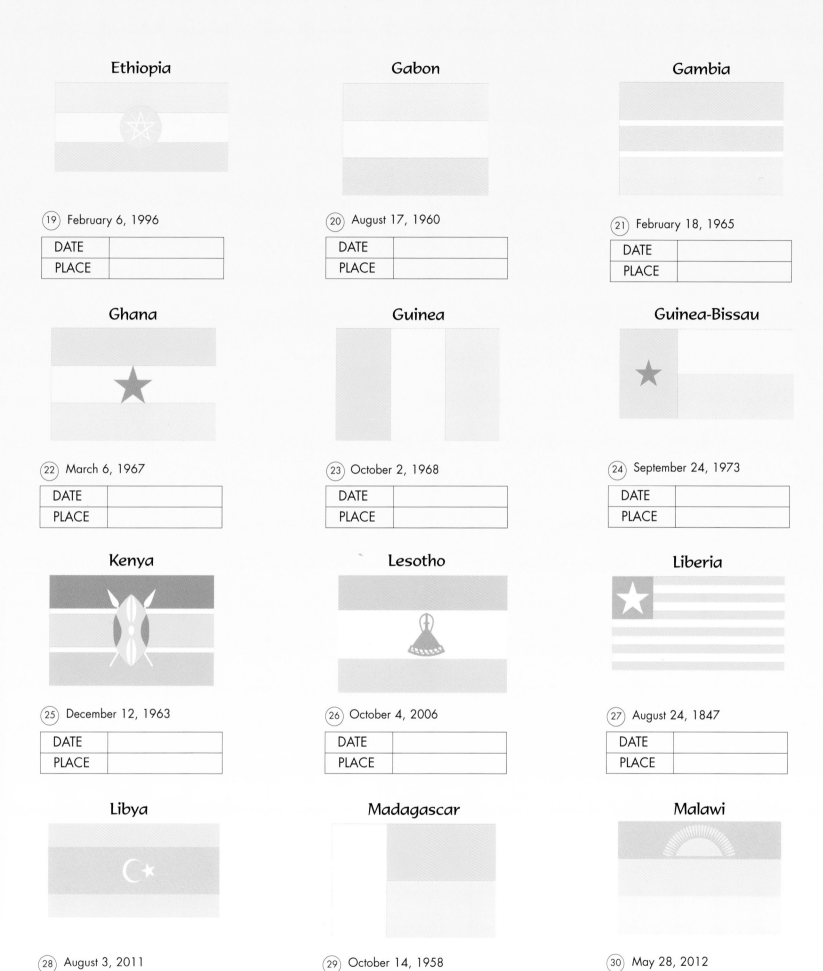

Ethiopia

⑲ February 6, 1996

DATE	
PLACE	

Gabon

⑳ August 17, 1960

DATE	
PLACE	

Gambia

㉑ February 18, 1965

DATE	
PLACE	

Ghana

㉒ March 6, 1967

DATE	
PLACE	

Guinea

㉓ October 2, 1968

DATE	
PLACE	

Guinea-Bissau

㉔ September 24, 1973

DATE	
PLACE	

Kenya

㉕ December 12, 1963

DATE	
PLACE	

Lesotho

㉖ October 4, 2006

DATE	
PLACE	

Liberia

㉗ August 24, 1847

DATE	
PLACE	

Libya

㉘ August 3, 2011

DATE	
PLACE	

Madagascar

㉙ October 14, 1958

DATE	
PLACE	

Malawi

㉚ May 28, 2012

DATE	
PLACE	

AFRICA

Mali

㉛ March 1, 1961

DATE	
PLACE	

Mauritania

㉜ April 1, 1959

DATE	
PLACE	

Mauritius

㉝ March 12, 1968

DATE	
PLACE	

Morocco

㉞ November 17, 1915

DATE	
PLACE	

Mozambique

㉟ May 1, 1983

DATE	
PLACE	

Namibia

㊱ March 21, 1990

DATE	
PLACE	

Niger

㊲ November 23, 1959

DATE	
PLACE	

Nigeria

㊳ October 1, 1960

DATE	
PLACE	

Rwanda

㊴ December 31, 2001

DATE	
PLACE	

São Tomé & Príncipe

㊵ July 12, 1975

DATE	
PLACE	

Senegal

㊶ August 20, 1960

DATE	
PLACE	

Seychelles

㊷ June 18, 1996

DATE	
PLACE	

Sierra Leone

(43) April 27, 1961

DATE	
PLACE	

Somalia

(44) October 12, 1954

DATE	
PLACE	

South Africa

(45) April 27, 1994

DATE	
PLACE	

South Sudan

(46) July 9, 2011

DATE	
PLACE	

Sudan

(47) May 20, 1970

DATE	
PLACE	

Swaziland

(48) October 30, 1967

DATE	
PLACE	

Tanzania

(49) June 30, 1964

DATE	
PLACE	

Togo

(50) April 27, 1960

DATE	
PLACE	

Tunisia

(51) July 3, 1999

DATE	
PLACE	

Uganda

(52) October 9, 1962

DATE	
PLACE	

Zambia

(53) October 24, 1964

DATE	
PLACE	

Zimbabwe

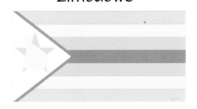

(54) April 18, 1980

DATE	
PLACE	

ASIA

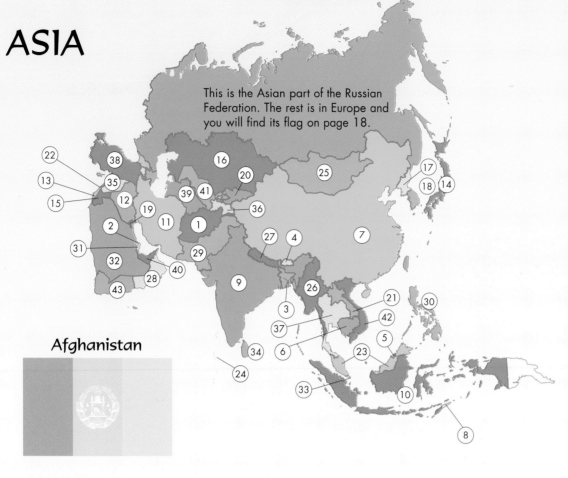

This is the Asian part of the Russian Federation. The rest is in Europe and you will find its flag on page 18.

Facts and figures

Area:
43.6 million square km
(16.8 square miles)

Total population:
4.1 billion*

Largest country: China
9.6 million square km
(3.7 million square miles)

Smallest country: Maldives
298 square km
(115 square miles)

Highest peak:
Mount Everest, Nepal
8,850m (29,030ft)

Longest river: Yangtze, China
6,380km (3,965 miles)

Biggest city:
Tokyo-Yokohama, Japan
Population 34 million†

Afghanistan

(1) January 4, 2004

DATE	
PLACE	

Bahrain

(2) February 16, 2002

DATE	
PLACE	

Bangladesh

(3) January 25, 1971

DATE	
PLACE	

Bhutan

(4) 1968

DATE	
PLACE	

Brunei

(5) September 29, 1959

DATE	
PLACE	

Cambodia

(6) June 29, 1993

DATE	
PLACE	

China

(7) October 1, 1949

DATE	
PLACE	

*Source: Population Reference Bureau, www.prb.org   †Source: www.citypopulation.de

East Timor (Timor-Leste)

8   May 20, 2002

DATE	
PLACE	

India

9   July 22, 1947

DATE	
PLACE	

Indonesia

10   August 17, 1945

DATE	
PLACE	

Iran

11   July 29, 1980

DATE	
PLACE	

Iraq

12   January 29, 2008

DATE	
PLACE	

Israel

13   October 28, 1948

DATE	
PLACE	

Japan

14   February 27, 1870

DATE	
PLACE	

Jordan

15   April 16, 1928

DATE	
PLACE	

Kazakhstan

16   June 4, 1992

DATE	
PLACE	

Korea, North

17   September 9, 1948

DATE	
PLACE	

Korea, South

18   January 25, 1950

DATE	
PLACE	

Kuwait

19   September 7, 1961

DATE	
PLACE	

ASIA

Kyrgyzstan

(20) March 3, 1992

DATE	
PLACE	

Laos

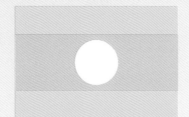

(21) December 2, 1975

DATE	
PLACE	

Lebanon

(22) December 7, 1943

DATE	
PLACE	

Malaysia

(23) September 16, 1963

DATE	
PLACE	

Maldives

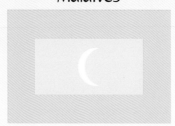

(24) July 12, 1965

DATE	
PLACE	

Mongolia

(25) February 12, 1992

DATE	
PLACE	

Myanmar (Burma)

(26) October 21, 2010

DATE	
PLACE	

Nepal

(27) December 16, 1962

DATE	
PLACE	

Oman

(28) April 25, 1995

DATE	
PLACE	

Pakistan

(29) August 11, 1947

DATE	
PLACE	

Philippines

(30) June 12, 1898

DATE	
PLACE	

Qatar

(31) July 9, 1971

DATE	
PLACE	

Saudi Arabia

(32) March 15, 1973

DATE	
PLACE	

Singapore

(33) December 3, 1959

DATE	
PLACE	

Sri Lanka

(34) December 27, 1951

DATE	
PLACE	

Syria

(35) March 29, 1980

DATE	
PLACE	

Tajikistan

(36) November 24, 1992

DATE	
PLACE	

Thailand

(37) September 28, 1917

DATE	
PLACE	

Turkey

(38) June 5, 1936

DATE	
PLACE	

Turkmenistan

(39) January 30, 1997

DATE	
PLACE	

United Arab Emirates

(40) December 2, 1971

DATE	
PLACE	

Uzbekistan

(41) November 18, 1991

DATE	
PLACE	

Vietnam

(42) November 30, 1955

DATE	
PLACE	

Yemen

(43) May 22, 1990

DATE	
PLACE	

OCEANIA

Indian Ocean

Pacific Ocean

Oceania is made up of hundreds of islands. Most of them are too small to be shown on this map.

Australia

(1) May 22, 1909

DATE	
PLACE	

Federated States of Micronesia

(2) November 30, 1978

DATE	
PLACE	

Fiji

(3) October 10, 1970

DATE	
PLACE	

Kiribati

(4) July 12, 1979

DATE	
PLACE	

Marshall Islands

(5) May 1, 1979

DATE	
PLACE	

Nauru

(6) January 31, 1968

DATE	
PLACE	

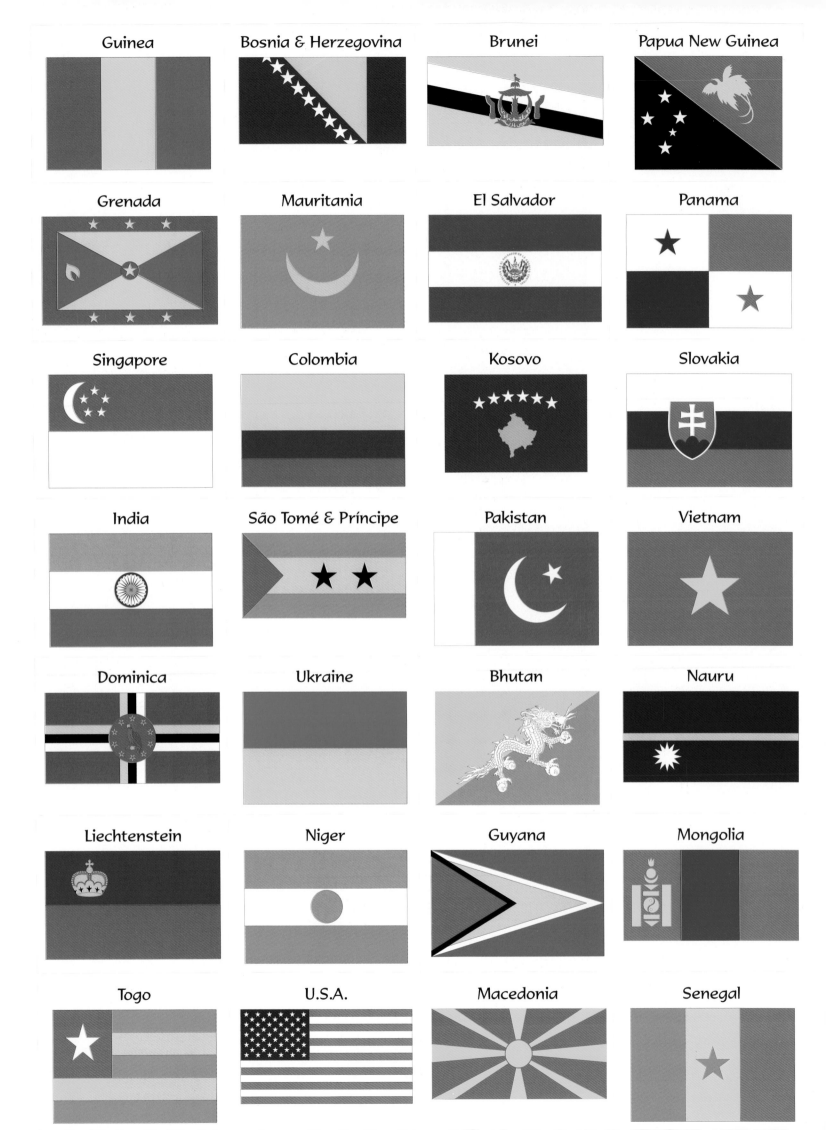

Guinea	Bosnia & Herzegovina	Brunei	Papua New Guinea
Grenada	Mauritania	El Salvador	Panama
Singapore	Colombia	Kosovo	Slovakia
India	São Tomé & Príncipe	Pakistan	Vietnam
Dominica	Ukraine	Bhutan	Nauru
Liechtenstein	Niger	Guyana	Mongolia
Togo	U.S.A.	Macedonia	Senegal

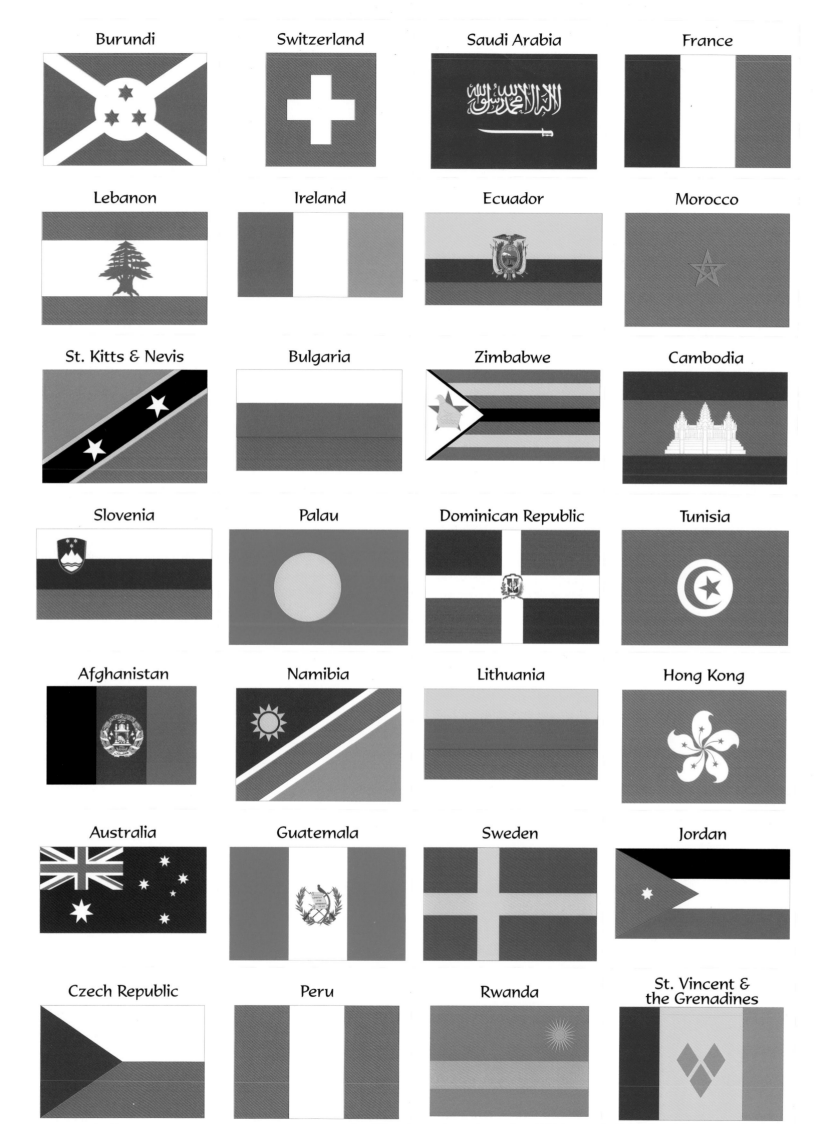

Burundi

Switzerland

Saudi Arabia

France

Lebanon

Ireland

Ecuador

Morocco

St. Kitts & Nevis

Bulgaria

Zimbabwe

Cambodia

Slovenia

Palau

Dominican Republic

Tunisia

Afghanistan

Namibia

Lithuania

Hong Kong

Australia

Guatemala

Sweden

Jordan

Czech Republic

Peru

Rwanda

St. Vincent &
the Grenadines

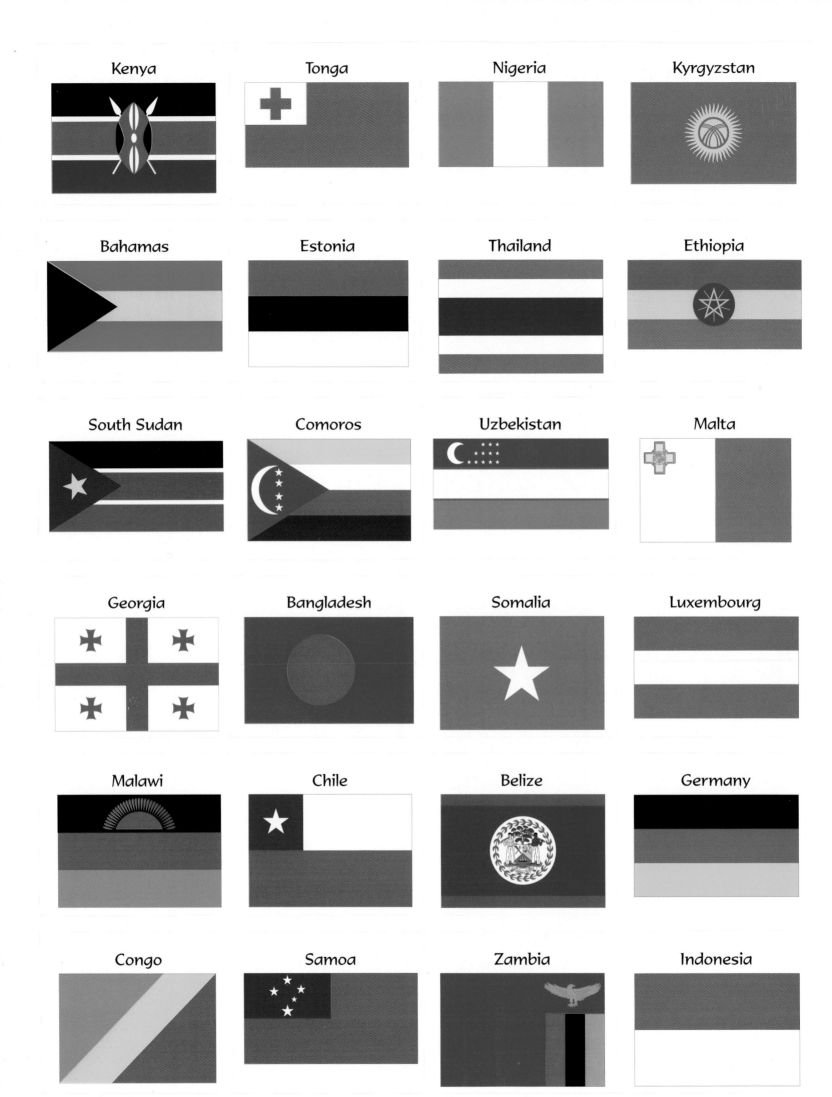

Kenya

Tonga

Nigeria

Kyrgyzstan

Bahamas

Estonia

Thailand

Ethiopia

South Sudan

Comoros

Uzbekistan

Malta

Georgia

Bangladesh

Somalia

Luxembourg

Malawi

Chile

Belize

Germany

Congo

Samoa

Zambia

Indonesia

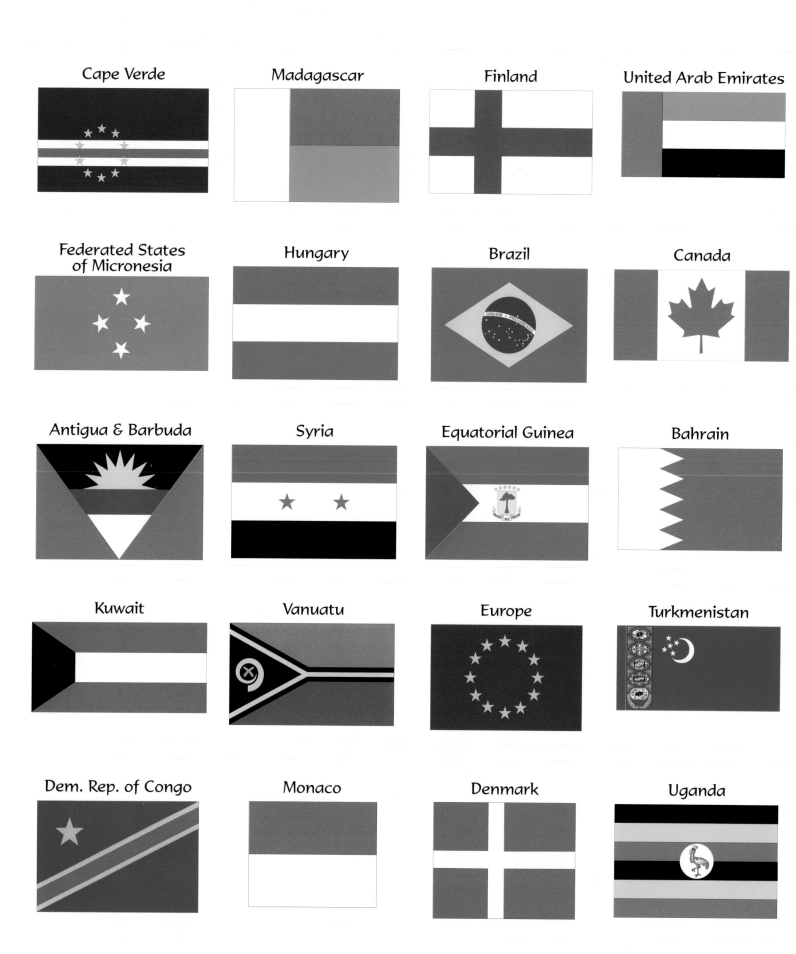

Cape Verde

Madagascar

Finland

United Arab Emirates

Federated States
of Micronesia

Hungary

Brazil

Canada

Antigua & Barbuda

Syria

Equatorial Guinea

Bahrain

Kuwait

Vanuatu

Europe

Turkmenistan

Dem. Rep. of Congo

Monaco

Denmark

Uganda

Chad

Mozambique

Serbia

Iran

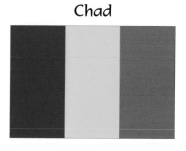

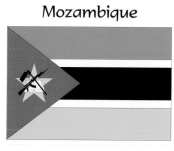

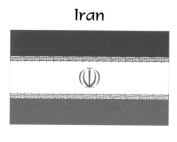

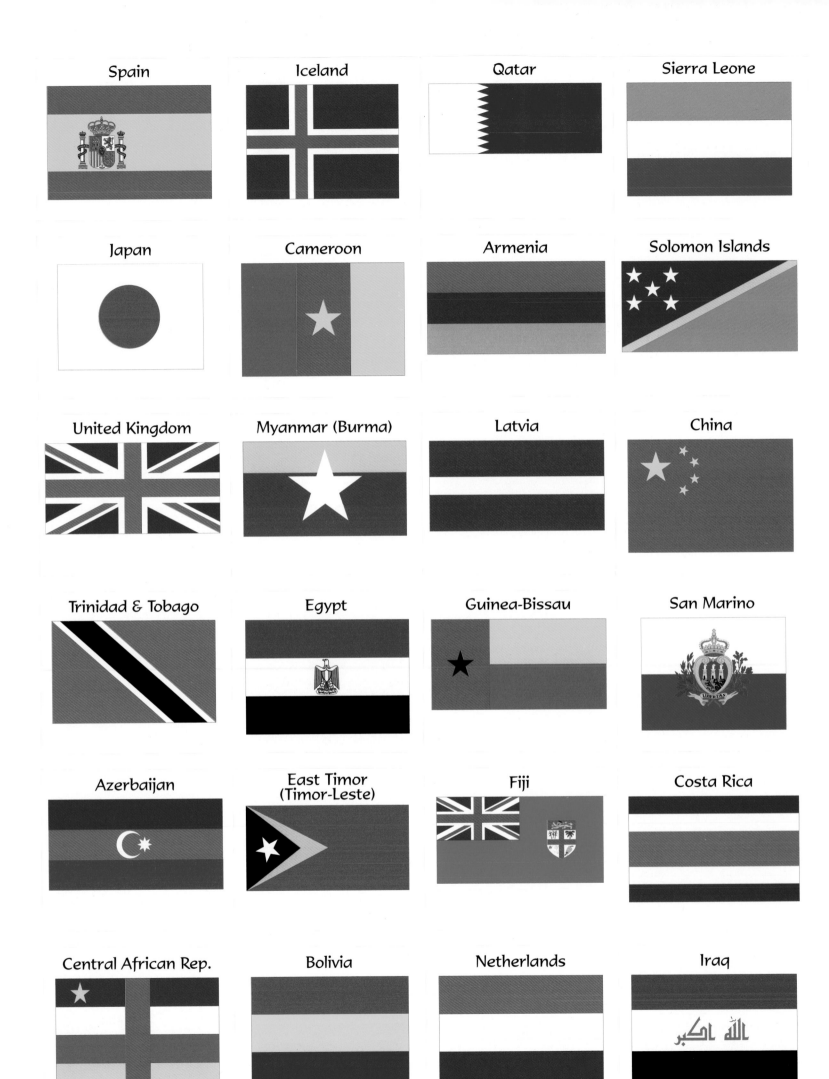

Spain

Iceland

Qatar

Sierra Leone

Japan

Cameroon

Armenia

Solomon Islands

United Kingdom

Myanmar (Burma)

Latvia

China

Trinidad & Tobago

Egypt

Guinea-Bissau

San Marino

Azerbaijan

East Timor (Timor-Leste)

Fiji

Costa Rica

Central African Rep.

Bolivia

Netherlands

Iraq

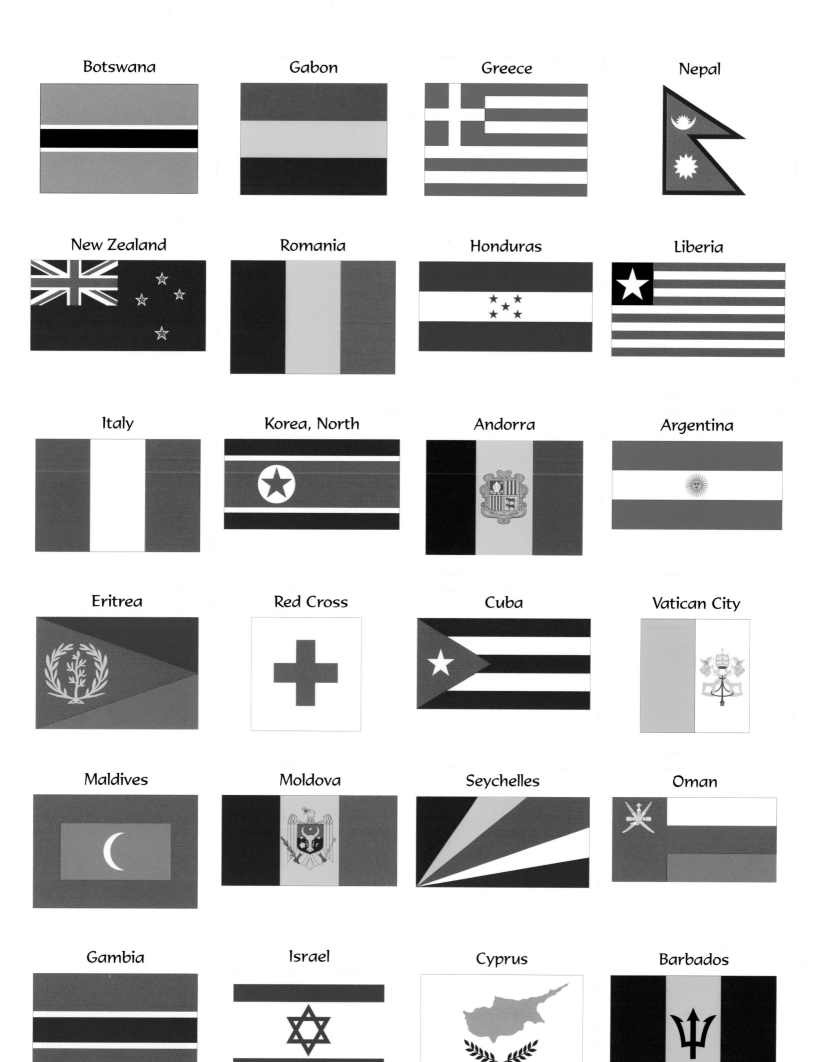

Angola Tuvalu Croatia South Africa

Montenegro Haiti Tanzania Philippines

Mali Albania Suriname Burkina Faso

Russian Federation NATO Malaysia St. Lucia

Mexico Ghana Paraguay Turkey

Laos Portugal Libya Austria

Algeria
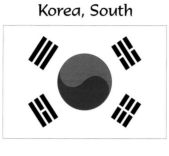

Belarus

Sri Lanka

Uruguay

Korea, South
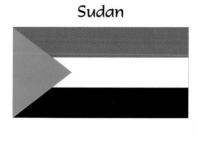

Jamaica
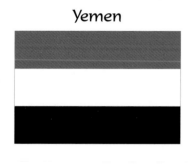

Côte d'Ivoire
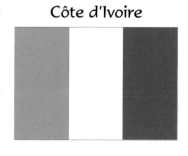

Poland

Sudan

Yemen

Red Crescent

Swaziland

Norway

Benin

Kiribati

Venezuela

Lesotho

Nicaragua

Belgium
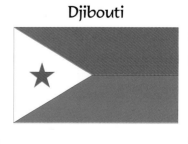

Kazakhstan

Mauritius
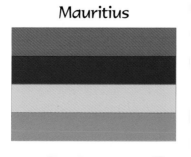

Tajikistan
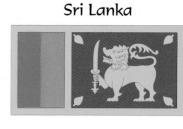

Djibouti

Marshall Islands

Facts and figures

Area:
9 million square km
(3.5 million square miles)

Total population: 36 million*

Largest country: Australia
7.7 million square km
(3 million square miles)

Smallest country: Nauru
21 square km
(8 square miles)

Highest peak: Mount Wilhelm,
Papua New Guinea
4,694m (15,400ft)

Longest river: Murray, Australia
3,680km (2,310 miles)

Biggest city: Sydney, Australia
Population 4.5 million†

Flag facts

The flags of many Oceanian countries feature either the United Kingdom's Union Jack flag or a pattern of stars called the Southern Cross constellation.

The Union Jack links the country with Britain – showing that it used to be part of the British Empire. The stars show that the country is in the Southern Hemisphere, because the Southern Cross constellation can only be seen in the night sky from the southern part of the world.

New Zealand

⑦ June 12, 1902

DATE	
PLACE	

Palau

⑧ January 1, 1981

PLACE	

Papua New Guinea

⑨ June 24, 1971

DATE	
PLACE	

Samoa

⑩ June 1, 1948

DATE	
PLACE	

Solomon Islands

⑪ November 18, 1977

DATE	
PLACE	

Tonga

⑫ 1866

DATE	
PLACE	

Tuvalu

⑬ October 1, 1996

DATE	
PLACE	

Vanuatu

⑭ February 18, 1980

DATE	
PLACE	

*Source: Population Reference Bureau, www.prb.org
†Source: www.citypopulation.de

EUROPE

Atlantic Ocean

This part of the Russian Federation is in Europe; the rest of it is in Asia.

Black Sea

Mediterranean Sea

Albania

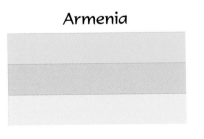

Andorra

Armenia

Austria

(1) April 7, 1992

DATE	
PLACE	

(2) June 20, 1996

DATE	
PLACE	

(3) August 24, 1990

DATE	
PLACE	

(4) November 11, 1918

DATE	
PLACE	

 *Source: Population Reference Bureau, www.prb.org
†Source: www.citypopulation.de

Facts and figures

Area:
10.5 million square km
(4.1 million square miles)

Total population:
738 million*

Largest country: Russian Fed.
17.1 million square km
(6.6 million square miles)

Smallest country:
Vatican City
0.44 square km
(0.17 square miles)

Highest peak:
Mount Elbrus, Russian Fed.
5,633m (18,476ft)

Longest river:
Volga, Russian Federation
3,688km (2,290 miles)

Biggest city:
Moscow, Russian Federation
Population 13.6 million†

Flag facts

The Scandinavian countries of Denmark, Sweden, Norway, Finland and Iceland all have flags that feature the "Scandinavian cross". This is a cross with arms of uneven length.

The flags of the Russian Federation, Croatia, the Czech Republic, Serbia, Slovenia and Slovakia all have sections of red, white and blue. This is to show that the people of these countries all share a common Slavic origin. The languages they speak – such as Russian, Czech and Serbian – are called Slavonic languages and are very closely related to each other.

The flags of France and the Netherlands were the original inspirations behind many of the three-striped flag designs adopted by countries all over the world.

Azerbaijan

⑤ February 5, 1991

DATE	
PLACE	

Belarus

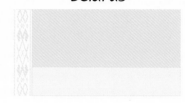

⑥ June 7, 1995

DATE	
PLACE	

Belgium

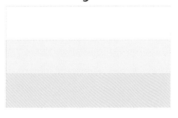

⑦ January 23, 1831

DATE	
PLACE	

Bosnia & Herzegovina

⑧ February 4, 1998

DATE	
PLACE	

Bulgaria

⑨ November 22, 1990

DATE	
PLACE	

Croatia

⑩ December 22, 1990

DATE	
PLACE	

Cyprus

⑪ August 16, 1960

DATE	
PLACE	

Czech Republic

⑫ March 30, 1920

DATE	
PLACE	

EUROPE

Denmark

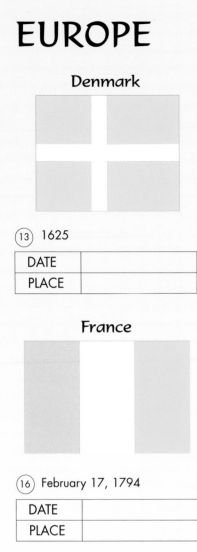

13 1625

DATE	
PLACE	

Estonia

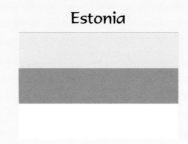

14 May 8, 1990

DATE	
PLACE	

Finland

15 May 29, 1918

DATE	
PLACE	

France

16 February 17, 1794

DATE	
PLACE	

Georgia

17 January 14, 2004

DATE	
PLACE	

Germany

18 May 23, 1949

DATE	
PLACE	

Greece

19 March, 1822

DATE	
PLACE	

Hungary

20 October 1, 1957

DATE	
PLACE	

Iceland

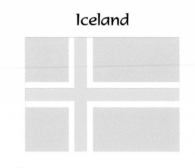

21 June 19, 1915

DATE	
PLACE	

Ireland

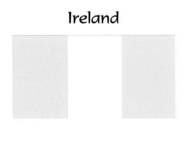

22 January 16, 1922

DATE	
PLACE	

Italy

23 June 18, 1946

DATE	
PLACE	

Kosovo

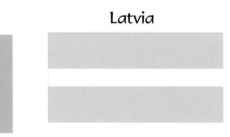

24 February 17, 2008

DATE	
PLACE	

Latvia

25 February 27, 1990

DATE	
PLACE	

Liechtenstein

(26) June 24, 1937

DATE	
PLACE	

Lithuania

(27) March 20, 1989

DATE	
PLACE	

Luxembourg

(28) August 16, 1972

DATE	
PLACE	

Macedonia

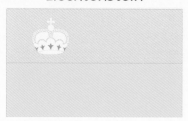

(29) October 5, 1995

DATE	
PLACE	

Malta

(30) September 21, 1964

DATE	
PLACE	

Moldova

(31) November 3, 1990

DATE	
PLACE	

Monaco

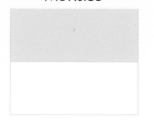

(32) April 4, 1881

DATE	
PLACE	

Montenegro

(33) June 3, 2006

DATE	
PLACE	

Netherlands

(34) February 19, 1937

DATE	
PLACE	

Norway

(35) January 1, 1899

DATE	
PLACE	

Poland

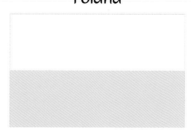

(36) November 11, 1918

DATE	
PLACE	

Portugal

(37) June 30, 1911

DATE	
PLACE	

EUROPE

Romania

(38) December 27, 1989

DATE	
PLACE	

Russian Federation

(39) December 22, 1991

DATE	
PLACE	

San Marino

(40) April 6, 1862

DATE	
PLACE	

Serbia

(41) June, 2006

DATE	
PLACE	

Slovakia

(42) September 1, 1992

DATE	
PLACE	

Slovenia

(43) June 24, 1991

DATE	
PLACE	

Spain

(44) October 28, 1981

DATE	
PLACE	

Sweden

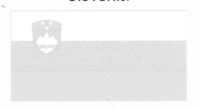

(45) June 22, 1906

DATE	
PLACE	

Switzerland

(46) December 12, 1889

DATE	
PLACE	

Ukraine

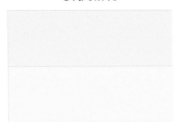

(47) September 4, 1991

DATE	
PLACE	

United Kingdom

(48) January 1, 1801

DATE	
PLACE	

Vatican City

(49) June 7, 1929

DATE	
PLACE	

NORTH AND CENTRAL AMERICA

Arctic Ocean

Pacific Ocean

Atlantic Ocean

Caribbean Sea

Facts and figures

Area:
25.4 million square km
(9.8 million square miles)

Total population: 515 million*

Biggest country: Canada
9.9 million square km
(3.8 million square miles)

Smallest country:
St. Kitts and Nevis
262 square km
(101 square miles)

Highest peak:
Mount McKinley, U.S.A.
6,194m (20,320ft)

Longest river:
Mississippi-Missouri, U.S.A.
6,020km (3,740 miles)

Biggest city:
Mexico City, Mexico
Population 22.7 million†

Flag facts

Many of the North and Central American countries have flags that are red, white and blue. This represents freedom and revolution and is based on the French flag, the Tricolore (see page 16).

Some of the flags on the next two pages are made up of blue and white stripes. These stripes show that the countries are part of Central America.

The flags of Jamaica, Dominica, and St. Kitts & Nevis all have sections of green, yellow and black. Green represents the countries' fertile land, yellow stands for sunshine and black represents the African heritage of their people.

*Source: Population Reference Bureau, www.prb.org
†Source: www.citypopulation.de

NORTH AND CENTRAL AMERICA

Antigua-Barbuda

① February 27, 1967

DATE	
PLACE	

Bahamas

② April 4, 1973

DATE	
PLACE	

Barbados

③ November 30, 1966

DATE	
PLACE	

Belize

④ September 21, 1981

DATE	
PLACE	

Canada

⑤ February 15, 1965

DATE	
PLACE	

Costa Rica

⑥ October 21, 1964

DATE	
PLACE	

Cuba

⑦ May 20, 1902

DATE	
PLACE	

Dominica

⑧ November 3, 1978

DATE	
PLACE	

Dominican Republic

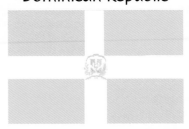

⑨ November 6, 1844

DATE	
PLACE	

El Salvador

⑩ September 14, 1972

DATE	
PLACE	

Grenada

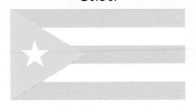

⑪ February 7, 1974

DATE	
PLACE	

Guatemala

⑫ December 26, 1997

DATE	
PLACE	

Haiti

⑬ February 25, 1986

DATE	
PLACE	

Honduras

⑭ February 16, 1866

DATE	
PLACE	

Jamaica

⑮ August 6, 1962

DATE	
PLACE	

Mexico

⑯ September 16, 1968

DATE	
PLACE	

Nicaragua

⑰ September 4, 1908

DATE	
PLACE	

Panama

⑱ November 3, 1903

DATE	
PLACE	

St. Kitts & Nevis

⑲ September 19, 1983

DATE	
PLACE	

St. Lucia

⑳ February 21,1967

DATE	
PLACE	

St. Vincent

㉑ October 21, 1985

DATE	
PLACE	

Trinidad & Tobago

㉒ June 8, 1962

DATE	
PLACE	

U.S.A.

㉓ July 4, 1960

DATE	
PLACE	

Flag facts

The stars featured on the flags of the U.S.A., Costa Rica, Dominica and Grenada represent areas within these countries – the fifty states of the U.S.A., the seven provinces of Costa Rica, the ten parishes of Dominica and the six parishes and capital city of Grenada.

SOUTH AMERICA

Caribbean Sea

Atlantic Ocean

French Guiana. This is not an independent country and does not have a flag of its own. It belongs to France, so it uses the French flag (see page 16).

Pacific Ocean

Atlantic Ocean

Facts and figures

Area:
17.6 million square km
(6.8 million square miles)

Total population: 386 million*

Largest country: Brazil
8.5 million square km
(3.3 million square miles)

Smallest country: Suriname
163,000 square km
(63,000 square miles)

Highest peak:
Aconcagua, Argentina
6,960m (22,828ft)

Longest river:
Amazon, Peru/Brazil
6,570km (4,080 miles)

Biggest city:
São Paulo, Brazil
Population 20.9 million†

Flag facts

The flags of Colombia, Ecuador and Venezuela are all made up of yellow, blue and red stripes. The yellow stripe symbolizes that these countries once belonged to a region called Greater Colombia. The blue stripe represents freedom, as the countries were once Spanish colonies, but then gained independence. The red stripe stands for the courage of their people in their fight for independence. The idea of using yellow, blue and red came from Francisco de Miranda, a nineteenth-century South American freedom fighter.

Freedom also inspired the design of Argentina's and Uruguay's flags. They both feature a sun emblem, which symbolizes independence from Spain.

*Source: Population Reference Bureau, www.prb.org
†Source: www.citypopulation.de

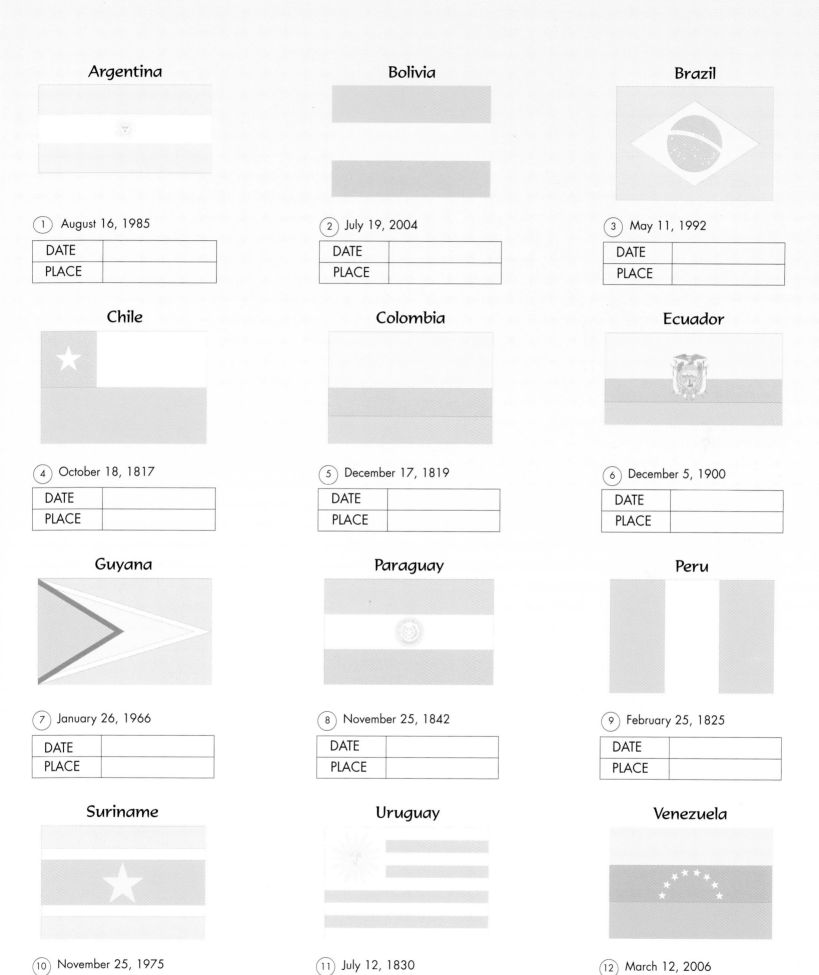

Argentina

① August 16, 1985

DATE	
PLACE	

Bolivia

② July 19, 2004

DATE	
PLACE	

Brazil

③ May 11, 1992

DATE	
PLACE	

Chile

④ October 18, 1817

DATE	
PLACE	

Colombia

⑤ December 17, 1819

DATE	
PLACE	

Ecuador

⑥ December 5, 1900

DATE	
PLACE	

Guyana

⑦ January 26, 1966

DATE	
PLACE	

Paraguay

⑧ November 25, 1842

DATE	
PLACE	

Peru

⑨ February 25, 1825

DATE	
PLACE	

Suriname

⑩ November 25, 1975

DATE	
PLACE	

Uruguay

⑪ July 12, 1830

DATE	
PLACE	

Venezuela

⑫ March 12, 2006

DATE	
PLACE	

INDEX

Material from www.prb.org is used with permission from the Population Reference Bureau (PRB), 1875 Connecticut Ave. NW, Suite 520, Washington DC 20009-5728 U.S.A. Not to be reproduced without permission from PRB.